THE BOSTON BRUINS

KURT WALDENDORF

childsworld.com

The Child's World®
childsworld.com

Published by The Child's World®
800-599-READ • www.childsworld.com

Photography Credits
Cover: ©Brian Fluharty/Getty Images; multiple pages: ©Hanna Siamashka/iStock/Getty Images; GLYPHstock/iStock/Getty Images; md tauhidul/Shutterstock; page 5: ©Steve Babineau/NHLI/Getty Images; page 6: ©Ray Lussier/MediaNews Group/Boston Record American/Boston Herald/Getty Images; page 9: ©Brian Babineau/NHLI/Getty Images; page 10: ©Jim Rogash/Getty Images; page 12: ©Steve Babineau/NHLI/Getty Images; page 12: ©John Russell/NHLI/Getty Images; page 13: ©Bruce Bennett Studios via Getty Images Studios/Getty Images; page 13: ©Minas Panagiotakis/Getty Images; page 14: ©Fred Kfoury III/Icon Sportswire/Getty Images; page 16: ©B Bennett/Getty Images; page 16: ©Bruce Bennett Studios via Getty Images Studios/Getty Images; page 17: ©Denis Brodeur/NHLI/Getty Images; page 17: ©Brian Babineau/NHLI/Getty Images; page 18: ©B Bennett/Bruce Bennett Studios via Getty Images Studios/Getty Images; page 18: ©UPI/Bettmann Archive/Getty Images; page 19: ©Elsa/Getty Images; page 19: ©Len Redkoles/NHLI/Getty Images; page 20: ©Len Redkoles/NHLI/Getty Images; page 20: ©Steve Babineau/NHLI/Getty Images; page 21: ©Dave Sandford/NHLI/Getty Images; page 21: ©Minas Panagiotakis/Getty Images; page 22: ©Focus on Sport/Getty Images; page 23: ©Minas Panagiotakis/Getty Images; page 25: ©Jim Rogash/Getty Images; page 26: ©Dan Goshtigian/The Boston Globe/Getty Images; page 29: ©Rich Lam/Getty Images

ISBN Information
9781503870710 (Reinforced Library Binding)
9781503871885 (Portable Document Format)
9781503873124 (Online Multi-user eBook)
9781503874367 (Electronic Publication)

LCCN
Library of Congress Control Number: 2024950386

Printed in the United States of America

BRINGING THE WORLD
19 68
TO YOUNG READERS

ABOUT THE AUTHOR

Kurt Waldendorf is the author of more than a dozen books for children. When he's not writing or editing, he enjoys indoor rock climbing and running along the shore of Lake Michigan with his dog. He lives in Chicago.

CONTENTS

Go Bruins!

The Boston Bruins compete in the National Hockey League's (NHL) Eastern Conference. They play in the Atlantic **Division** with the Buffalo Sabres, Detroit Red Wings, Florida Panthers, Montreal Canadiens, Ottawa Senators, Tampa Bay Lightning, and Toronto Maple Leafs. The Bruins are the third-oldest team in the NHL. They have played more than 100 seasons. Bruins fans have been lucky! The Bruins have appeared in the NHL **playoffs** 77 times. The team has won six Stanley Cups. Let's learn more about the Bruins.

Eastern Conference • Atlantic Division

Boston Bruins	Buffalo Sabres	Detroit Red Wings	Florida Panthers
Montreal Canadiens	Ottawa Senators	Tampa Bay Lightning	Toronto Maple Leafs

Boston fans are eager for their team to win a seventh Stanley Cup, but they show up to cheer for the Bruins no matter where they rank.

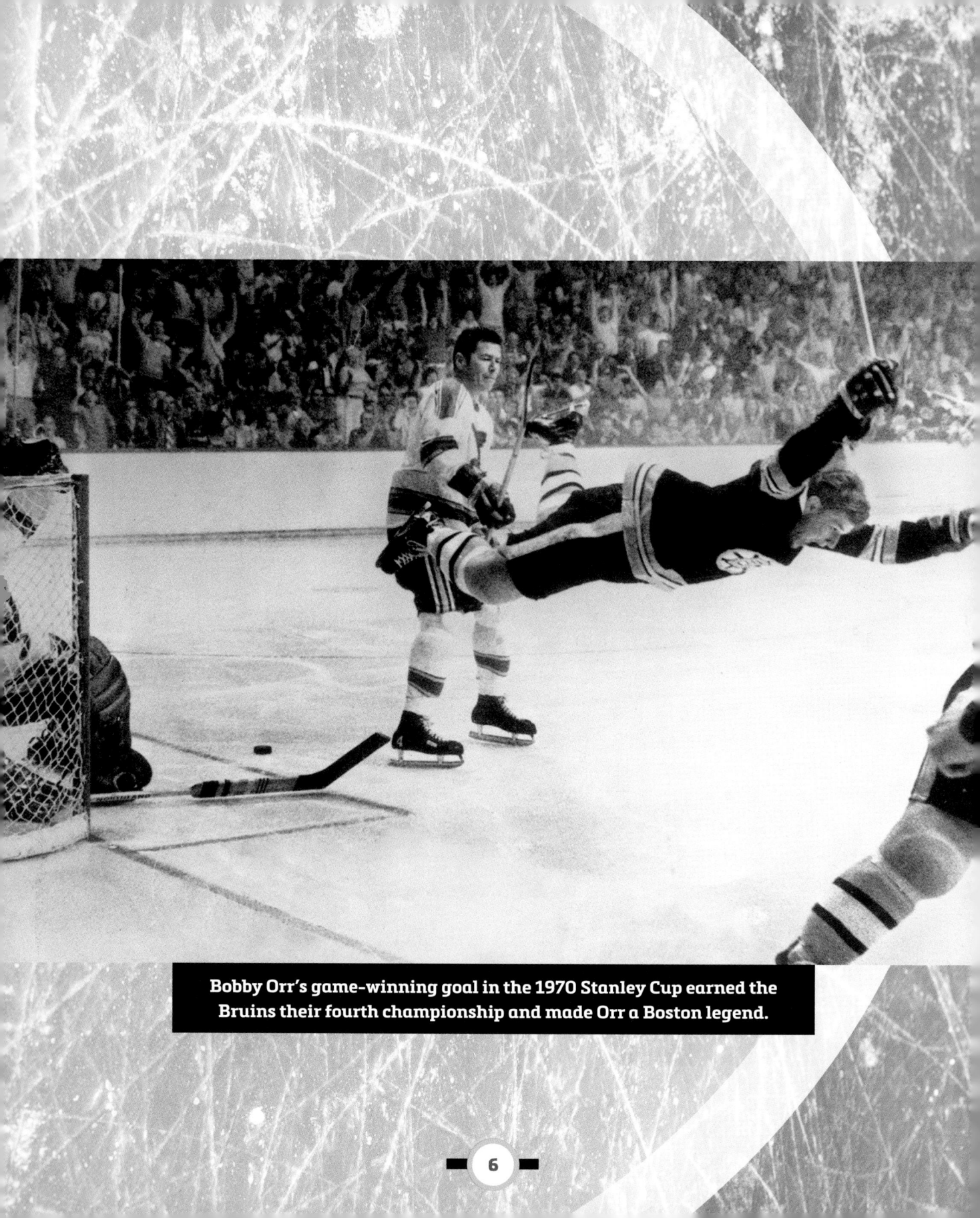

Bobby Orr's game-winning goal in the 1970 Stanley Cup earned the Bruins their fourth championship and made Orr a Boston legend.

Becoming the Bruins

In 1924, the Boston Bruins became the first US team in the NHL. Led by **Hall of Fame**-bound players Eddie Shore, Aubrey "Dit" Clapper, and Cecil "Tiny" Thompson, the team found early success. Boston won three Stanley Cups from 1929 to 1941. In the 1960s, the Bruins were one of the worst teams in the NHL. Then, Bobby Orr and Phil Esposito joined the team. They led the Bruins to Stanley Cup wins in 1970 and 1972. Defenseman Ray Bourque joined the team in 1979. He helped the Bruins reach the playoffs a record 29-straight seasons. But the Bruins did not win any more championships. Finally in 2011, center Patrice Bergeron and goalie Tim Thomas led the team to its sixth Stanley Cup. In recent years, wingers Brad Marchand and David Pastrňák stepped up to keep the Bruins among the league's top teams.

By the Numbers

The Bruins have had a lot of success on the ice. Below is some information about the team's success throughout history:

The Bruins have won the Stanley Cup six times.

6

The team has earned a total of 30 division titles.

30

The Bruins hold the record for most wins in a season, with 65.

65

The Bruins have reached the playoffs 77 times.

77

Tyler Seguin raises the team's sixth Stanley Cup. The Bruins and the Chicago Blackhawks are tied for fourth-most Stanley Cup wins.

TD Garden holds 17,850 screaming Bruins fans for hockey games, and another 1,300 for basketball games.

Game Night

For almost 70 years, the Bruins played in the Boston Garden. The stadium was known for having seats close to the ice. Fans cheered loudly, giving the Bruins a home-ice advantage. In 1995, the Bruins moved to TD Garden. The team shares the arena with the Boston Celtics of the National Basketball Association. Some days, both teams play in the arena. Workers can change the basketball court to an ice rink in about two hours. TD Garden also hosts concerts as well as figure skating, gymnastics, and tennis events. Each year, about 3.5 million people visit the arena.

We're Famous!

Members of the American rock band the Dropkick Murphys are big Bruins fans. The band's song "Time to Go" cheers the team on, saying, "Go! Go! Black and gold!" and "Drop the puck, it's time to go." In 2010, the band performed at Boston's first Winter Classic, a special NHL game held outdoors. The Bruins have also partnered with the band to raise money for charity.

Uniforms

HOME

AWAY

Goalie Mask

NHL goalies started wearing masks in the 1950s. For years, the masks were plain white with holes cut out for the players' eyes. In the late 1960s, Bruins goalie Gerry Cheevers started decorating his mask. He drew stitches in the places where pucks had struck. Other goalies started decorating their masks, too. Goalie masks have changed a lot since Cheevers' time. So have the designs. In the late 1980s and early 1990s, Bruins goalie Andy Moog became known for his "Big Bad Bruin" mask. It featured a snarling brown bear above the face shield.

Truly Weird

The Bruins' name and colors have a strange history. Charles Adams bought the team in 1924. Adams also owned grocery stores. When it was time to pick the team's colors, he chose the colors commonly used in his stores: brown and yellow. For a team name, he wanted a brown animal to match. He chose an old-fashioned name for brown bears: Bruins. Eventually, the team's colors changed to black and gold. The logo became a black-and-gold wheel with a letter "B" in the middle. This represents Boston's nickname of "The Hub." But Adams's team name has remained unchanged.

Team Spirit

Boston fans are passionate about their team. Nearly 18,000 people pack TD Garden for each home game. Blades the Bruin has been the team's mascot since 1999. Before the puck drops, Blades gets everyone fired up from the stands. A famous person, usually an athlete or celebrity, waves a Bruins flag. The fans sometimes pass a giant Bruins banner around the arena. When the Bruins score a goal, a foghorn sounds. The crowd chants as music plays. Near the end of the game, fans often sing along to the song "Livin' on a Prayer" by the band Bon Jovi. The music gives the team a boost of energy to finish the game strong.

When he is not hyping up fans during home games, Blades the Bruin visits hospitals and other locations in the Boston area.

Heroes of History

Johnny Bucyk
Left Winger | 1957–1978

Johnny Bucyk is not the flashiest player in Bruins history. But the large winger was a steady presence for the Bruins for 21 seasons. Alongside greats such as Bobby Orr and Phil Esposito, Bucyk helped lead the team to Stanley Cup wins in 1970 and 1972. By the time of his retirement in 1978, Bucyk had racked up 545 goals, the most ever by a Bruins player. Today, he is a member of the Hockey Hall of Fame. He still works for the Bruins as a team ambassador.

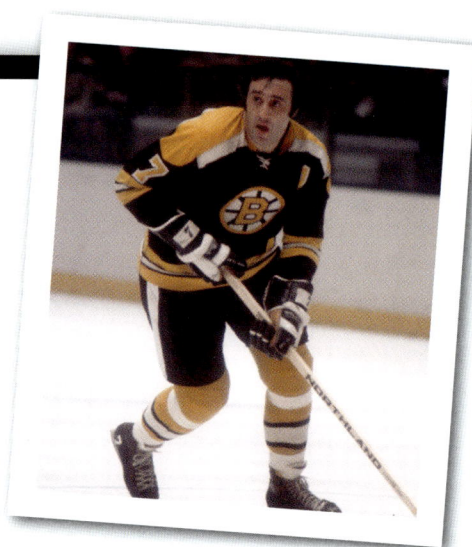

Phil Esposito
Center | 1967–1975

Phil Esposito was one of the top scorers of his time. He used his size and strength to stay in front of the other team's net. When a puck would bounce off the goalie, Esposito would be there to knock it into the goal. In 1969, Esposito became the first player to score more than 100 points in a season. In 1971, he scored a record 76 goals and 152 points. Only three players have scored more goals in a season. Esposito is a member of the Hockey Hall of Fame.

Ray Bourque
Defenseman | 1979–2000

For more than 20 years, Ray Bourque was the heart of the Bruins' lineup. He led the team to the playoffs 17-straight seasons from 1980 to 1996. He was named the league's top defenseman five times. But he never won a Stanley Cup with the Bruins. He was traded to the Colorado Avalanche in 2000. When he won a title with the Avalanche in 2001, Boston fans held a rally for him. Bourque holds NHL records for the most goals, assists, and points by a defenseman. He is a member of the Hockey Hall of Fame.

Patrice Bergeron
Center | 2003–2023

Patrice Bergeron played his whole career with the Bruins. Across 19 seasons, he became known as one of the best two-way players ever. That means he was great at both scoring and defending. In 2011, he scored the winning goal in Game 7 of the Stanley Cup Final. The win gave Boston its first title since 1972. It also made Bergeron a member of the Triple Gold Club. He won an Olympic gold medal, a World Championship gold medal, and a Stanley Cup in his career.

Big Days

APRIL 12, 1941

Led by Hall of Famer Aubrey "Dit" Clapper, the Bruins beat the Detroit Red Wings four games to none in the Stanley Cup Final. It is Boston's second title in three years and third overall.

After finishing first and second in the league in goals, Phil Esposito, Bobby Orr, and Johnny Bucyk help the Bruins win their fifth Stanley Cup. It is also the team's second Cup in three seasons.

MAY 11, 1972

JUNE 15, 2011

The Bruins capture their sixth Stanley Cup title and their first in 39 years. Bruins goalie Tim Thomas is named the playoffs' Most Valuable Player (MVP).

The Bruins set the NHL record for wins in a season with 65. In the same game, David Pastrňák scores his 61st goal of the season.

APRIL 13, 2023

Modern-Day Marvels

David Pastrňák
Right Winger | 2014–Present

David "Pasta" Pastrňák is a veteran leader for the Bruins. Selected in the 2014 NHL Draft, Pastrňák grew up playing hockey in the Czech Republic. He quickly made a name for himself as a scorer in the NHL. The trio of Pastrňák, Patrice Bergeron, and Brad Marchand became known as The Perfection Line for their balanced play. In 2020, Pastrňák scored 48 goals. He tied Washington Capitals star Alex Ovechkin for the most in the league. In 2023, Pastrňák scored an outstanding 61 goals, the most for a Bruin since 1975.

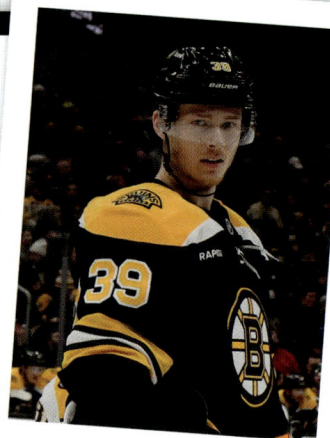

Morgan Geekie
Center | 2019–Present

Morgan Geekie started his NHL career with the Carolina Hurricanes. He scored two goals in his first game. Geekie moved on to the Seattle Kraken and logged 16 goals and 34 assists over two seasons. In 2023, he joined the Boston Bruins and continued to make in impact on the ice. Geekie scored his first hat trick and his 100th career point with the Bruins and was one of the team's top scorers at the start of the 2024–25 season. His younger brother Conor also plays in the NHL.

Charlie McAvoy
Defenseman | 2017–Present

Charlie McAvoy joined the Bruins during the 2017 playoffs. He made a difference right away, filling in for injured defensemen. The following season, McAvoy scored 32 points and was named to the NHL All-Rookie team. Then in 2019, he scored eight points in the playoffs to help the Bruins get to the Stanley Cup Final. Today, McAvoy is one of the top defensemen in the league. In addition to scoring, he is one of the team's leaders in ice time, hits, and blocked shots.

Jeremy Swayman
Goaltender | 2020–Present

Jeremy Swayman is an up-and-coming star with the Bruins. In 2022, he split playing time with veteran goalie Linus Ullmark. Swayman was named to the NHL All-Rookie team. The next year, the two goalies dominated. They won the William M. Jennings Trophy, which is given to the team's goalies that allow the fewest goals in a season. In 2024, Ullmark was traded to another team, and Swayman took over. The future looks bright with the young star in the net.

Bobby Orr scored 888 points, including 624 assists, during his 10 seasons with the Bruins.

The G.O.A.T.

Bobby Orr did everything for the Bruins. He led the team to Stanley Cup wins in 1970 and 1972. He was named the league's MVP three times. He was picked as the NHL's top defender eight years in a row from 1968 to 1975. On offense, Orr won the league's scoring title two times. No other defenseman has won the scoring title. At age 31, Orr became the youngest player ever selected for the Hockey Hall of Fame. Orr still holds the records for most points and assists in a season by a defenseman.

Fan Favorite

Zdeno Chára played for the Bruins from 2006 to 2020. At 6 feet, 9 inches (2.1 meters) tall, Chára was known for his size and strength. But it was his toughness that made him a fan favorite. During the 2019 Stanley Cup Final, Chára took a puck to his face. His jaw was broken. But he finished the series anyway. As Chára skated onto the ice in the next game, the crowd greeted him with a roar.

The Big Game

The 2010 playoffs were heartbreaking for Bruins fans. The team was up three games to zero in their playoff series against the Philadelphia Flyers. Then, the Bruins collapsed. The team lost four-straight games and was knocked out of the tournament. The following year, the Bruins faced off against their biggest **rival**, the Montreal Canadiens, in the first round of the playoffs. After losing the first two games in the series at home, it looked like it might be another disappointing playoff exit for the Bruins. But this time, Boston battled back. In Game 7, the Bruins and Canadiens went into **overtime**. Bruins winger Nathan Horton knocked in the winning goal. The Bruins went on to hoist its first Stanley Cup in nearly 40 years.

Nathan Horton celebrates his three game-winning goals with teammate Milan Lucic during the 2011 NHL playoffs. ▶

Phil Esposito scored 459 total goals during his nine seasons with the Bruins.

Amazing Feats

Shutouts
Hal Winkler tallied 15 **shutouts** in 1927–1928, the most in Bruins history.

15

Penalty Minutes
In the 1987–1988 season, winger Jay Miller racked up a total of 304 penalty minutes.

304

Defenseman Points
In 1970–1971, defenseman Bobby Orr scored 37 goals and had 102 assists. His 139 points are the most ever by a defenseman.

139

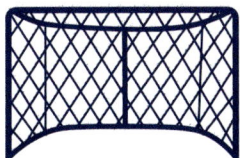

Power Play Goals
Center Phil Esposito knocked in 27 **power play** goals on the way to a Stanley Cup title in 1972. He later matched his own team record in the 1974–1975 season.

27

All-Time Best

MOST POINTS

1	Ray Bourque	1,506
2	Johnny Bucyk	1,339
3	Patrice Bergeron	1,040
4	Phil Esposito	1,012
5	Brad Marchand	976

HAT TRICKS

1	Phil Esposito	26
2	David Pastrňák	17
3	Cam Neely	14
4	Johnny Bucyk	12
5	Bobby Orr	9

MOST GOALS

1	Johnny Bucyk	545
2	Phil Esposito	459
3	Patrice Bergeron	427
4	Brad Marchand	422
5	Rick Middleton	402

SAVES

1	Tuukka Rask	14,345
2	Eddie Johnston	12,375
3	Gerry Cheevers	10,579
4	Tim Thomas	10,533
5	Byron Dafoe	6,401

MOST ASSISTS

1	Ray Bourque	1,111
2	Johnny Bucyk	794
3	Bobby Orr	624
4	Patrice Bergeron	613
5	David Krejčí	555

SHUTOUTS

1	Cecil "Tiny" Thompson	74
2	Tuukka Rask	52
3	Frank Brimsek	35
4	Tim Thomas	31
5	Eddie Johnston	27

Tuukka Rask was known as The Great Wall during his 15 NHL seasons, all with the Bruins.

GLOSSARY

ambassador (am-BAS-uh-dur) An ambassador is a person who speaks for or represents an organization.

division (dih-VIZSH-un) A division is a group of teams within the NHL that compete with each other to have the best record each season and advance to the playoffs.

draft (DRAFT) A draft is a yearly event when teams take turns choosing new players. In the NHL, teams can select North American ice hockey players between the ages of 18 and 20, and international players between 18 and 21 to join the league.

Hall of Fame (HAHL of FAYM) The Hockey Hall of Fame is a museum in Ontario, Canada. The best players and coaches in the game are honored there.

line (LINE) A line in hockey is made up of a center, left winger, and right winger who are on the ice at the same time.

overtime (OH-vur-tym) Overtime is extra time added to the end of a game when the regular time is up and the score is tied.

playoffs (PLAY-offs) Playoffs are games that take place after the end of the regular season to determine each year's championship team.

power play (POW-uhr PLAY) A power play occurs when a player gets a penalty and the other team has more players on the ice.

retirement (ree-TY-uhr-ment) Retirement occurs when an athlete chooses to end their competitive playing career.

rival (RYE-vuhl) A rival is a team's top competitor, which they try to outdo and play better than each season.

rookie (ROOK-ee) A rookie is a new or first-year player in a professional sport.

shutout (SHUT-owt) A shutout occurs when a goalie keeps the other team from scoring any goals.

FAST FACTS

- Charles Francis Adams paid $15,000 for the team in 1924. The team is now worth around $2.67 billion.

- The Bruins played their first games in Matthews Arena in 1924. The arena is the oldest ice hockey rink in the world and is still used today.

- The Bruins were the first NHL team to have a Black player on their roster. In 1958, Willie O'Ree broke the NHL's color barrier.

- The Bruins are tied with the Chicago Blackhawks for the fourth-most Stanley Cups. Only the Detroit Red Wings, Toronto Maple Leafs, and Montreal Canadiens have more.

ONE STRIDE FURTHER

- Ray Bourque played for 21 seasons with the Bruins and easily holds the career record for points. Phil Esposito played with the team for only nine seasons but holds the top five records for goals scored in a season. Which accomplishment do you think is more impressive and why?

- Based on what you've learned from this book, what do you think it takes for a team to win the Stanley Cup? Is it great scoring? Excellent defenders? A top goalie? What about leadership? Discuss your opinion with a friend.

- Players around the world train hard to make it to the NHL. Write a paragraph describing the skills and attitudes you think it takes to reach the highest level.

- Ask friends and family members to name their favorite sport to watch and their favorite sport to play. Keep track and make a graph to see which sports are the most popular.

FIND OUT MORE

IN THE LIBRARY

Fickett, Jamie. *The Boston Bruins vs. The Montreal Canadiens.*
Coral Springs, FL: Seahorse, 2024.

Graves, Will. *Pro Hockey Upsets.* Minneapolis, MN: Lerner, 2020.

Laughlin, Kara L. *Hockey.* Parker, CO: The Child's World, 2024.

Orr, Bobby and Kara Kootstra. *Bobby Orr and the Hand-Me-Down Skates.*
Toronto, ON: Tundra, 2020.

ON THE WEB

Visit our website for links about the Boston Bruins:
childsworld.com/links

Note to Parents, Caregivers, Teachers, and Librarians: We routinely verify our web links to make sure they are safe and active sites. So encourage your readers to check them out!

INDEX